Sarah McLachlan

Song Book Designed by John Rummen & Crystal Heald
Line Art Drawings by Sarah McLachlan
Cover Photography by Al Robb
Live Shots by Steve Jennings & Al Robb
Song Sheet Photography by Kharen Hill
  Crystal Heald & Rapheal Mazzuco
Plenty Drawing by Graham Gilmore
Back Cover Photo Kharen Hill

HAL•LEONARD CORPORATION

7777 W. BLUEMOUND RD. P.O. BOX 13819 MILWAUKEE, WI 53213

Born on January 28th, 1968, Sarah McLachlan has reached a level of artistic maturity that takes most artists years to attain. Since releasing **Touch** in 1988, the Halifax, Nova Scotia native has explored her own unique musical interests, indifferent to current trends and fads. Sarah's intimate vocals and moody evocative songs convey a passionate honesty not found in most of today's music.

Sarah studied classical guitar and piano as a child and at the age of 17 was discovered by Nettwerk Records at her first performance as part of a New Wave band. Reluctant parents kept Sarah from signing her first record deal for two years. After relocating to Vancouver, Sarah began writing music for her first album **Touch**. Much to Sarah's surprise, the album went GOLD in Canada and she was suddenly rocketed to stardom while being hailed as the year's most exciting and important new artist.

After an extensive tour with her first band, Sarah returned to the studio to record **Solace**, which was released in 1991. **Solace** succeeded critically and commercially and catapulted Sarah to international prominence:

" ... astonishing strength and clarity ... "
Rolling Stone Magazine

" Sarah McLachlan will be around for a while ... trust your ears."
New York Daily News

The release of **Solace** was followed by an exhaustive 14 month tour, after which Sarah returned to Vancouver to begin writing the songs for her latest album **Fumbling Towards Ecstasy**.

With the release of **Fumbling**, Sarah has unveiled a more personal album - the culmination of six months in a Montréal studio with long-time friend and producer, Pierre Marchand. Her latest release reflects the many changes Sarah has undergone since the release of **Solace**. Sarah describes the writing of **Fumbling** as "a kind of therapy," a process which enabled her to overcome many long standing fears and concerns by articulating them in her music. Metaphorically **Fumbling** represents the stripping away of the things that prevent us from achieving happiness and fulfillment.

The songs on **Fumbling** examine issues of self-deception and self-actualization from many different perspectives. *Possession*, the album's dark and driving lead track was written from the perspective of obsessive fans. It examines a fan's overwhelming need to control someone they know only through music. Blind promises of love are intertwined with images of desperation and violence to create a tense and threatening mood which is underscored by the track's propulsive rhythm and raw guitar.

Hold On, was inspired by the documentary, **A Promise Kept**, about a woman whose fiancé discovers he has AIDS. Overwhelmed by the woman's strength and selflessness, Sarah wrote the song in a single day. It is an unsentimental portrait of a woman's courage in the face of adversity. *Hold On* also appears on the **No Alternative** compilation album (a follow-up to the very successful **Red, Hot & Blue** and **Red, Hot & Dance** compilations). The proceeds from all three compilations go to support AIDS research.

Fumbling's lighter side represents a departure for Sarah. "Before I didn't want to write when I was happy ... It was almost as if I needed to be depressed in order to be creative." *Ice Cream*, which contains the phrase "your love is better than ice cream," shows Sarah's new found ability to find inspiration through happiness as well as sadness. Part of Sarah's artistic and personal maturation has been learning to enjoy the good things in life. Still though, *Ice Cream* is tempered by a feeling of the fear of rejection or loss; "It's a long way down," she warns in the chorus.

After the whirlwind existence Sarah has lived for the last few years, she is learning to savour the few precious moments of privacy and calm that she gets. While recording **Fumbling** Sarah rented a secluded house in the woods outside of Montréal. At first the solitude and lack of distraction were unsettling but the natural beauty of the setting eventually soothed and inspired her.

"I love to listen to the river ... It's the best music I've heard in years."

For more information, please contact **Nettwerk Productions**. Box 330-1755 Robson Street, Vancouver, B.C., Canada V6G 3B7 Tel:(604) 654-2929 Fax:(604) 654-1993 Email: nettwerk@mindlink.bc.ca Nettwerk Electronic BBS (604) 731-7007

Ben's Song

On the hills of fire the darkest hour
I was dreaming of my true loves' bower
Who will bring a light to stoke the fire
Fear not for you're still breathing

   On a windless day I saw the life blood drained away

    A cold wind blows on a windless day

Hear the cry for new life the mournings flame
You were the brightest light that burned too soon in vain
Who will bring you back from where there's no return
Fear not for your just dreaming

   On a windless day I saw the life blood drained away

A cold wind blows on a windless day.

BEN'S SONG

Words and Music by
SARAH McLACHLAN

MCA music publishing

To Coda I

Fear _____ not for you're still breath - ing. __
Fear _____ not for you're just dream - ing. __

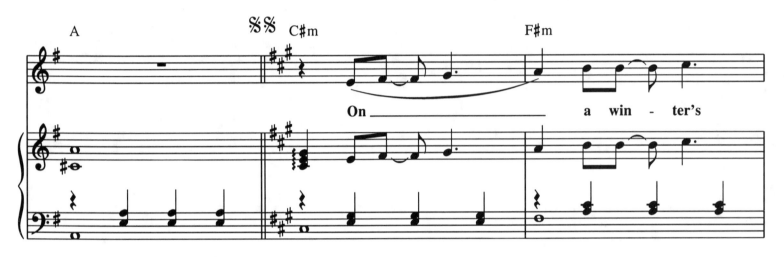

On _____ a win - ter's

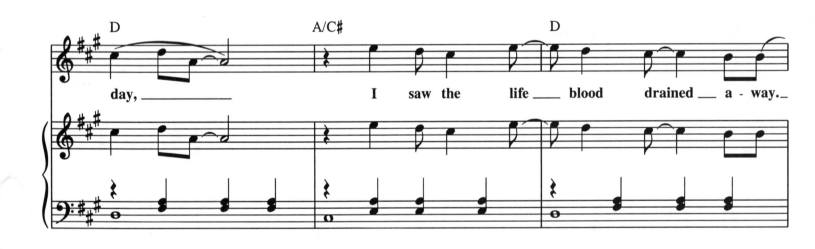

day, _____ I saw the life __ blood drained __ a - way.

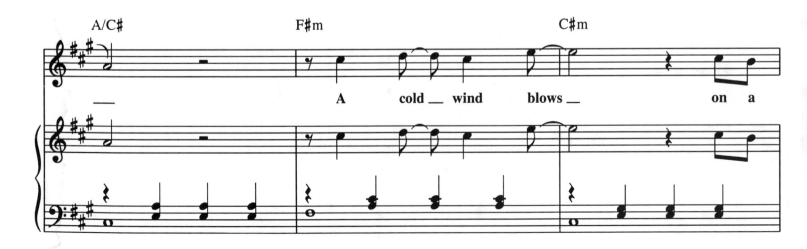

__ A cold __ wind blows __ on a

CODA II

Vox

In the desert of my dreams I saw
you there & I'm walking towards the
water steaming body cold & bare.
But your words cut loose the fire &
you left my soul to bleed & the pain
that's in your truth: decieving me has
got me scared oh why? Oh why?
Through your eyes the stains of
battle like a brooding storm: you
up & down these pristine velvet
walls like focus never forms. My
walls are getting wider & my eyes
are drawn astray. I see you now
a vague deception of a dying day
Oh why? Oh why? I fall into the
water & once more I turn to you:
& the crowds were standing staring
faceless cutting off my view to you.
They start to limply flail their
bodies in a twisted mime & I'm
lost inside this tangled web in
which I'm lain entwined. You're
gone & I'm lost inside this tangled
web & which I'm lain entwined
Oh why? Oh why?

VOX

Words and Music by
SARAH McLACHLAN

MCA music publishing

Drawn to the Rhythm

When we wore a heart of stone we wandered to the sea. Hoping to find some comfort there yearning to feel free & we were mesmerised by the lull of the night & the smells that filled the air & we laid us down on sandy ground it was cold but we didn't care & we were drawn to the rhythm. drawn into the rhythm of the sea yes we were drawn to the rhythm. drawn into the rhythm of the sea. We fell asleep & began to dream when something broke the night. Memories stirred inside of us the struggle & the fight & we could feel the heat of a thousand voices telling us which way to go & we cried out is there no escape from the words that plague us so & we were drawn to the rhythm. drawn into the rhythm of the sea yes we were drawn to the rhythm. drawn into the rhythm of the sea. In the still & the silent dawn another day is born. Washed up by the tireless waves the body bent & torn. In the face of the blinding sun awake only to find that heaven is a stranger place than the one I've left behind & we were drawn to the rhythm. drawn into the rhythm of the sea. we were drawn to the rhythm drawn into the rhythm of the sea ...

DRAWN TO THE RHYTHM

Words and Music by
SARAH McLACHLAN

MCA music publishing

CODA

Verse

Path of Thorns

I knew you wanted to tell me. In your voice there was something wrong. but if you would turn your face away from me· you cannot tell me you're so strong· Just let me ask of you one small thing· as we have shared so many tears· With fervor our dreams we planned a whole life long· now are scattered on the wind· In the terms of endearment· In the terms of the life that you loved·in the terms of the years that passed you by· In the terms of the reasons why· Through the years I've grown to love you·though your commitment to most would offend but I stuck by you holding on with my foolish pride· waiting for you to give in You never really tried or so it seemed I've had much more than myself to blame I've had enough of trying everything·This time it is the end· Chorus· There's no more coming back this way· The path is over grown & strewn with thorns· They've torn the life blood from your naked eyes·cast aside to be forlorn· Chorus· funny how it seems that all I've tried to do· Seems to make no difference at all at all...

THE PATH OF THORNS (TERMS)

Words and Music by
SARAH McLACHLAN

Bridge

Fun-ny, how __ it seems __ that all __ I've tried __ to do __ seemed to make __ no dif - fer - ence to you, at all. __

Instrumental ad lib. and Fade

Outro

Repeat ad lib. and Fade

I Will Not Forget You

I remember the nights I watched as you
lay sleeping. Your body gripped by some far away
dream. Well I was so scared & so in love then. And
so lost in all of you that I had seen. But no one ever
talked in the darkness. no voice ever offered fuel to the
fire. No light ever shone in the doorway. Deep in
the hollows of earthly desires. But if in some
dream there was brightness. If in some memory
some sort of sign & flesh be revived in the
shadows. Blessed our bodies would lay so
entwined. And I will oh I will not forget you.
Nor will I ever let you go. I will oh I will not forget
you. I remember when you left in the morning at day-
break. Oh, so silent you stole from my bed. to go back
to the one who possessed your soul & I back to the life that
I dread. So I ran like the wind to the water. Please don't
leave me again I cried & I threw bitter tears at the
ocean but all that came back was the tide.
I will oh I will not forget you. Nor will I ever
let you go. I will oh I will not forget
you. Nor will I ever let you go
I will oh I will not forget you.

I WILL NOT FORGET YOU

Words and Music by SARAH McLACHLAN
and DARREN PHILLIPS

Bridge

no one ev - er talked in the dark-ness.
if in some dream there was bright-ness,
ran like the wind to the wa - ter.

No voice ev - er add - ed fuel __
if in some mem - o - ry
Please, don't leave me a -

__ to the fire.
some sort of sigh,
- gain, I cried.

No light ev - er shone in the door - way,
and flesh be re - vived in the shad - ows,
And I threw bit - ter tears at the o - cean, but

deep in the hol - low of earth - ly de - sires. But
bless - ed, our bod - ies would
all that came back was the

lay so en - twined. And

Chorus

I will, __ oh, I will __ not _____ for - get you,

CODA II

Lost

By the shadows of the
Night I go. I move away from
the crowded room. That sea
of shallow faces marked in
warm regret. They don't know
how to feel. They don't know what
is lost. Lost in the darkness
of a land. Where all the hope
that's offered is. Memories of
being taken by the hand. And
We are led into the sun. But I
don't have a hold on what is real
Though we can only try. What is
there to give or to believe. I
want it all to go away I want
to be alone. Sympathy's wasted
on my hollow shell. I feel there's
nothing left to fight for. No
reason for a cause. I can't
hear your voice. I can't
feel you near. Chorus.
I wanted a change know-
ing all I could do was
try. I was looking for
Some One ...

LOST

Words and Music by
SARAH McLACHLAN

MCA music publishing

Possession

Listen as the wind blows from across the great divide. Voices trapped in yearning memories draped in time. The night is my companion solitude my guide. Would I spend forever here & not be satisfied ? I would be the one to hold you down kiss you so hard I'll take your breath away & after I'd wipe away the tears just close your eyes dear. Through this world I've stumbled so many times betrayed. Trying to find an honest word to find the truth enslaved. Oh you speak to me in riddles oh you speak to me in rhyme. My body aches to breathe your breath your words keep me alive. & I would be the one to hold you down kiss you so hard I'll take your breath away & after I'd wipe away the tears just close your eyes dear. Into this night I wander it's morning that I dread. Another day of knowing of the path I fear to tread. Oh into the sea of waking dreams I follow without pride. nothing stands between us here & I won't be denied. & I would be the one to hold you down kiss you so hard I'll take your breath away & after I'd wipe away the tears just close your eyes...

POSSESSION

Words and Music by
SARAH McLACHLAN

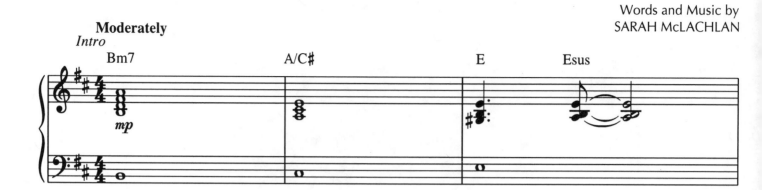

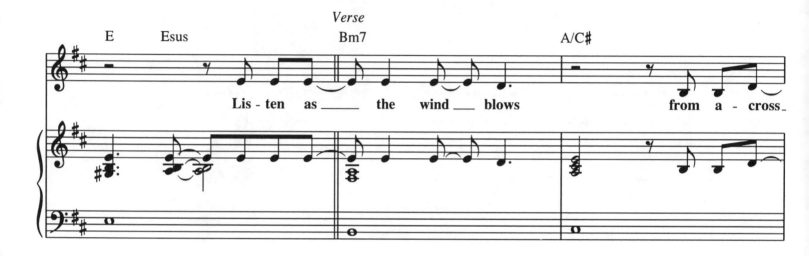

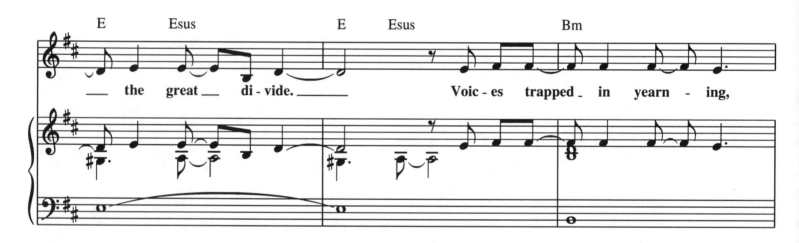

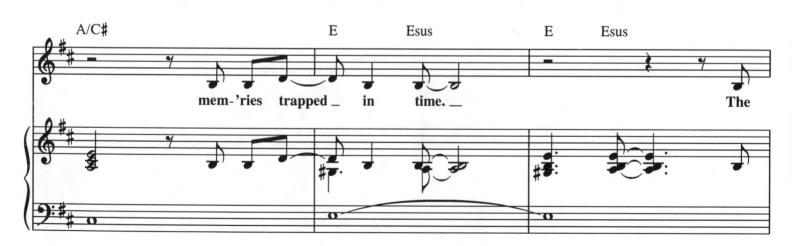

Wait

Under a blackend sky far beyond the glaring street lights. sleeping on empty
dreams the vultures lie in wait. You lay down beside me then you were with
me every waking hour so close I could feel your breath. When all we
wanted was the dream to have & to hold that precious little thing like
every generation yields a newborn hope unjaded by their years. Pressed
up against the glass I found myself wanting sympathy but to be consum
again oh I know would be the death of me. There is a love that's
inherently given. A kind of blindness offered to appease & in that
light of forbidden joy oh I know I wont recieve it. When all we
wanted was the dream to have & to hold that precious little thing
like every generation yields a newborn hope unjaded by their years.
You know if I leave you now it doesn't mean I love you any less
it's just the state I'm in I cant be good to anyone else like this
When all we wanted was the dream to have & to hold that precious
little thing like every generation yields a newborn hope unjaded by
their years.

WAIT

Words and Music by
SARAH McLACHLAN

Quietly

Un - der a black - ened sky, ___
Pressed up a - gainst the glass, ___

Instrumental solo

Good Enough

Hey your glass is empty it's a hell of a long way home. Why dont you let me take you it's no good to go alone. I never would have opened up but you seemed so real to me. & after all the bull shit I've heard it's refreshing not to see I dont have to pretend she doesn't expect it from me. So dont tell me I haven't ~~been~~ good to you dont tell me I haven't been there for you just tell me why nothing is good enough

Hey little girl would you like some candy your mama says it's ok. The door is open come on outside No I cant come out today. It's not the wind that cracked your shoulder & threw you to the ground. Who's there that makes you so afraid your shaken to the bone & I dont understand you deserve so much more than this. So dont tell my why he's never been good to you dont tell me why he's never been there for you dont you know that why is simply not good enough oh so just let me try & I will be good to you just let me try & I will be there for you I'll show you why your so much more than good enough.

GOOD ENOUGH

Words and Music by
SARAH McLACHLAN

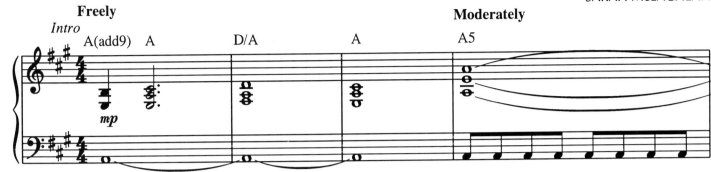

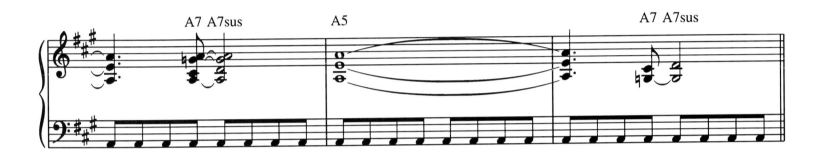

Hey, your glass is emp-ty; it's a hell of a long way home.
Hey, lit-tle girl, would you like some can-dy? Your mom-ma said that it's o-kay.

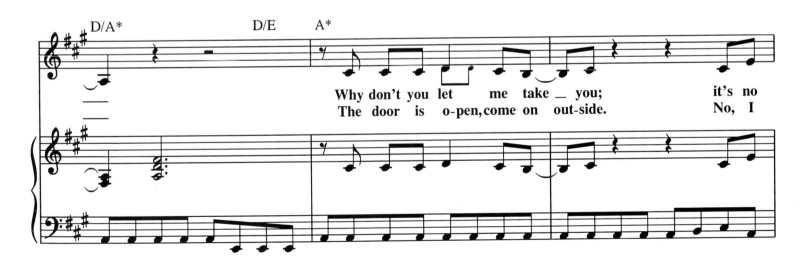

Why don't you let me take you; it's no
The door is o-pen, come on out-side. No, I

and I will be there _ for _ you. I'll show you why _ you're so much more than

good e-nough. *Guitar solo*

Circle

There are two of us talking in circles & one of us who wants to leave. In a world created for only us an empty cage that has no key. Dont you know that we're working with flesh & blood carving out of jealousy. Crawling into each other it's smothering every little part of me. What kind of love is this that keeps me hanging on despite everything it's doing to me. What is this love that keeps me coming back for more when it will only end in misery. I know too many people unhappy in a life from which they'd love to flee. watching others get everything offered they're wanton for discovery. Oh my brother my sister my mother your losing your identity dont you know that It's you in the window shinning with intensity. What kind of love is this that keeps me hanging on despite everything It's doing to me. What is this love that keeps me coming back for more when it will only end in misery.

CIRCLE

Words and Music by
SARAH McLACHLAN

Elsewhere

I love this time of in between. the calm inside me. in the space where I can breathe I believe there is a distance I have wandered to touch upon the years of reaching out reaching in holding out holding in. I believe this is heaven to no one else but me & I'll defend it long as I can be left here to linger in silence if I choose to would you try to understand. I know this love is passing time passing through like liquid I am drunk in my desire. but I love you smile at me I love the way your hands reach out & hold me near. I believe. I believe this is heaven to no one else but me & I'll defend it as long as I can be left here to linger in silence if I choose to would you try to understand. Oh the quiet child awaits the day when she can break free the mold that clings like desperation. Mother cant you see I've got to live my life the way I feel is right for me might not be right for you but it's right for me. I believe. I believe this is heaven to no one else but me & I'll defend it as long as I can be left here to linger in silence if I choose to would you try to understand. Yeah I would like to linger here in silence if I choose to would you understand it would you try.

ELSEWHERE

Words and Music by
SARAH McLACHLAN

*Vocal written one octave higher than sung.

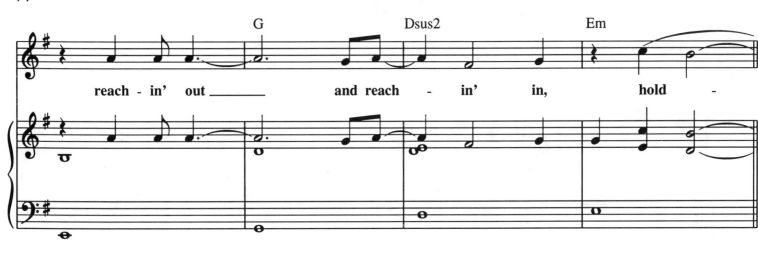

reach - in' out _____ and reach - in' in, hold -

Chorus

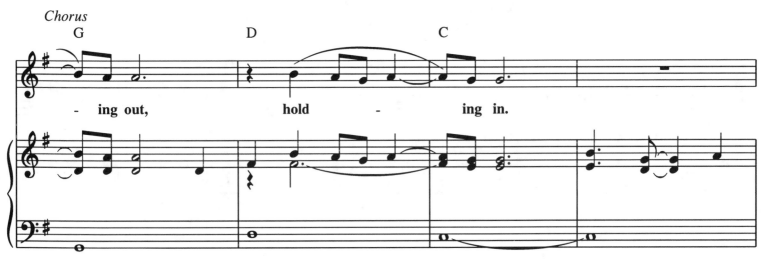

- ing out, hold - ing in.

I _____ be - lieve _____ this is heav -

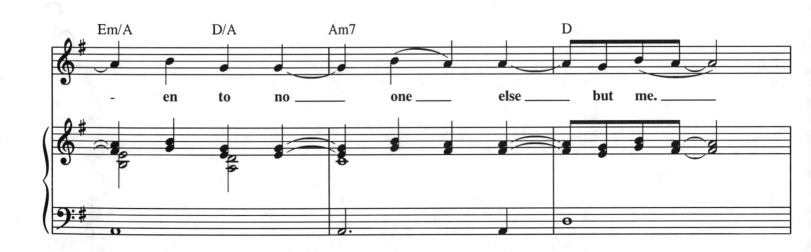

- en to no _____ one _____ else _____ but me. _____

Mary

Mary walks down to the waters edge : there she hangs her head
to find herself faded a shadow of what she once was. She says
"How long have I been sleeping : why do I feel so old why do I
feel so cold. My heart is saying one thing but my body wont let
go." With trembling hands she reaches up a strangers flesh is offered
: I would be the last to know I would be the last to let it show
I would be the last to go. Take her hand she will lead you through
the fire : give you back hope : hope that you wont take too
much respecting what is left She cradled us eh she held us
in her arms unselfish in her suffering she could not understand
that no one seems to have the time to cherrish what is offered
: I would be the last to know I would be the last to let it
show I would be the last to go.

MARY

Words and Music by
SARAH McLACHLAN

* Chords in parentheses are
played on 2nd verse.

Hold On

Hold on hold on to yourself for this is gonna hurt like hell. Hold on hold on to yourself you know that only time will tell. What is it in me that refuses to believe this isn't easier than the real thing. My love you know that you're my best friend you know I'd do anything for you ∴ my love but nothing come between us my love for you is strong ∴ true Am I in heaven here or am I ...? at the crossroads I am standing New you're sleeping peaceful I lie awake ∴ pray that you'll be strong tomorrow ∴ We will see another day ∴ we will praise it ∴ love the light that brings a smile across your face. Oh god if you're out there won't you hear me I know that we've never talked before but oh god the man I love is leaving won't you take him when he comes to your door. Am I in heaven here or am I in hell at the crossroads I am standing. ∴ New you're sleeping peaceful I lie awake ∴ pray that you'll be strong tomorrow ∴ we will see another day ∴ we will praise it ∴ love the light that brings a smile across your face. Hold on. hold on to yourself for this is gonna hurt like hell.

HOLD ON

Words and Music by
SARAH McLACHLAN

CODA

love the light __ that brings __ a smile __ a - cross __ your

__ face.

Hold on. _____ Hold on to your - self, __

__ for this is gon - na hurt like _____ hell.

Ice

The ice is thin come on dive in underneath my lucid skin the
cold is lost forgotten. Hours pass days pass time stands still
light gets dark & darkness fills my secret heart forbidden...
I think you worried for me then the subtle ways that I'd give
in but I know you liked the show & tied down to this bed of
shame You tried to move around the pain but oh your soul
is anchored. The only comfort is the moving of the river. You
enter into me a lie upon your lips. offer what you can I'll take
all that I can get only a fool's here... I don't like your tragic
sighs as if your god has passed you by well hey fool that's your
deception. Your angels speak with jilted tongues the serpent's
tale has come undone you have no strength to squander.
The only comfort is the moving of the river. You enter into me
a lie upon your lips. offer what you can I'll take all that I can
get only a fool's here to stay... only a fool's here...

ICE

Words and Music by
SARAH McLACHLAN

Ice Cream

Your love is better than ice cream better than anything else that I've
tried. Your love is better than ice cream & everyone here knows how to
fight. & it's a long way down. it's a long way down. it's a long way
down to the place where we started from. Your love is better than
chocolate better than anything else that I've tried your love is
better than chocolate & everyone here knows how to cry & It's a
long way down It's a long way down It's a long way down to the
place where we started from.

ICE CREAM

Words and Music by
SARAH McLACHLAN

Moderately Fast

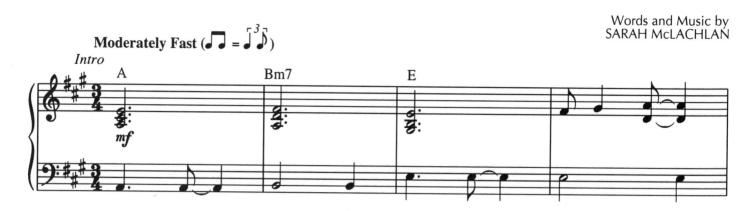

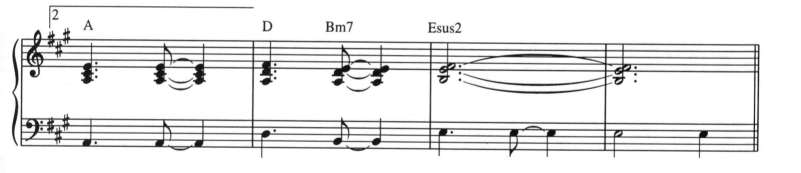

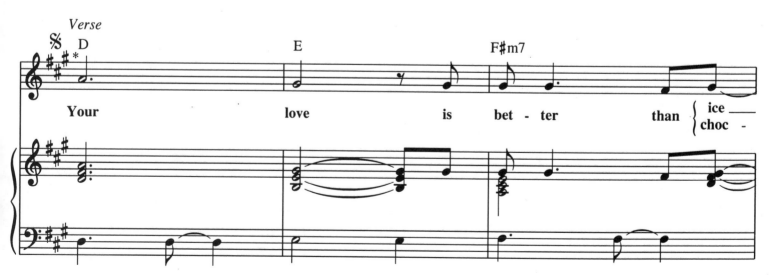

Your love is bet - ter than ice choc -

Vocal written one octave higher than sung.

Fear

Morning smiles like the face of a newborn child innocent unknowing.
Winter's end promises of a long lost friend speaks to me of comfort.
but I fear I have nothing to give I have so much to lose here in this
lonely place tangled up in our embrace there's nothing I'd like better
than to fall. but I fear. I have nothing to give. Wind in time rapes the
flower trembling on the vine i nothing yields to shelter it. from above
they say temptation will destroy our love. the never ending hunger. But
I fear. I have nothing to give. I have so much to lose here in this
lonely place tangled up in your embrace there's nothing I'd like
better than to fall. But I fear. I have nothing to give. I have
so much to lose. I have nothing to give. We have so much to lose.

FEAR

Words and Music by
SARAH McLACHLAN

Chorus

But I

- ing.
- fort.

fear   I have noth - ing to give. ___ I

have so much to lose ___ here in ___ this lone - ly place; _ tan -

- gled up ___ in ___ your ___ em - brace. _ There's noth-ing I'd ___ like bet -

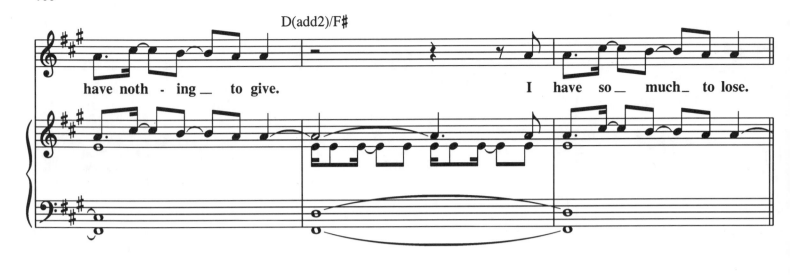

Additional Lyrics

3. Wind in time rapes the flower
   trembling on the vine
   And nothing yields to shelter it from above.

4. They say temptation will destroy our love
   The never ending hunger
   (But I fear. . .)

Plenty

I looked into your eyes they told me plenty I already knew. You never felt a thing so soon forgotten all that you do. In more than words I tried to tell you the more I tried I failed. I would not let myself believe that you might stray & I would stand by you no matter what they'd say I thought I'd be with you until my dying day until my dying day. I used to think my life was often empty a lonely space to fill. You hurt me more than I ever could have imagined. You made my world stand still. But in that stillness there was a freedom I never felt before. I would not let myself believe that you might stray & I would stand by you no matter what they'd say. I thought I'd be with you until my dying day until my dying day.

PLENTY

Words and Music by
SARAH McLACHLAN

Moderately

Intro

Play 4 times

Verse

I looked in - to ___ your ___ eyes;
I used to think ___ my ___ life

they told me plen - ty
was of - ten emp - ty,

I al - lone -

- ly read - y knew.
space to fill.

You
You

Fumbling Towards Ecstasy

All the fear has left me now I'm not frightened anymore. It's my heart that pounds beneath my flesh. It's my mouth that pushes out this breath ; If I shed a tear I wont cage it. I wont fear love ; if I feel a rage I wont deny it. I wont fear love. Companion to our demons they will dance ; we will play. With chairs, candles ; cloth making darkness in the day. It'll be easy to look in or out. upstream or down without a thought ; If I shed a tear I wont cage it. I wont fear love ; if I feel a rage I wont deny it. I wont fear love ; If I shed a tear I wont cage it. I wont fear love ; if I feel a rage I wont deny it I wont fear love I wont fear love I wont fear love ...

FUMBLING TOWARDS ECSTASY

Words and Music by SARAH McLACHLAN
and PIERRE MARCHAND

BEN'S SONG
(Guitar Part)

Words and Music by
SARAH McLACHLAN

C   G   D   A   E7   G/A   C#m   F#m   A/C#

VOX
(Guitar Part)

Words and Music by
SARAH McLACHLAN

C   Fmaj7   Am7   G   Gsus   G/A   D7   F   C*

Intro
Moderately

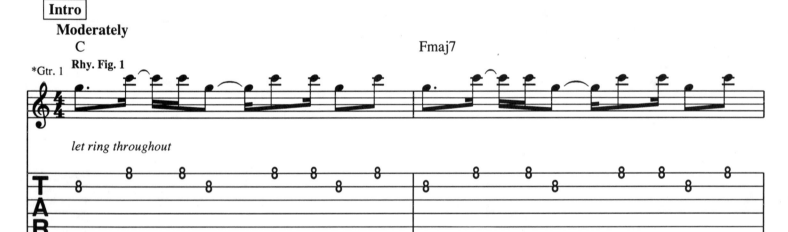

*Gtr. 1 — Rhy. Fig. 1

let ring throughout

* 12-str. acous.

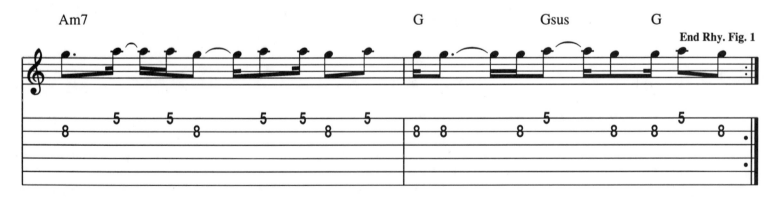

End Rhy. Fig. 1

Verse
w/ Rhy. Fig. 1, 3 times

C   Fmaj7   Am7   G

Play 3 times

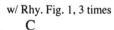

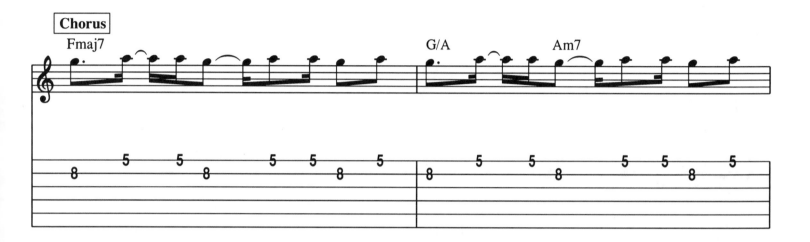

Chorus

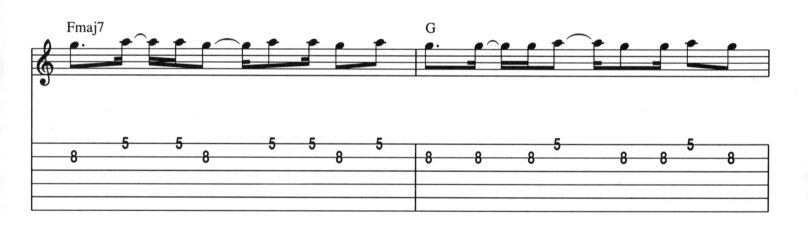

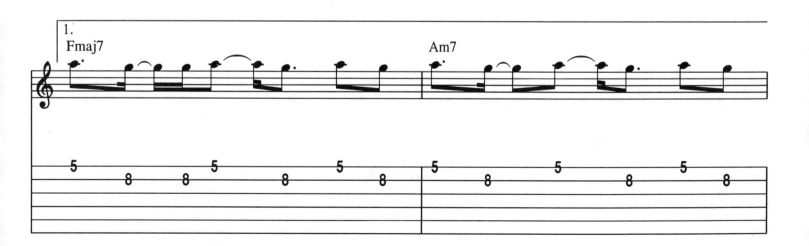

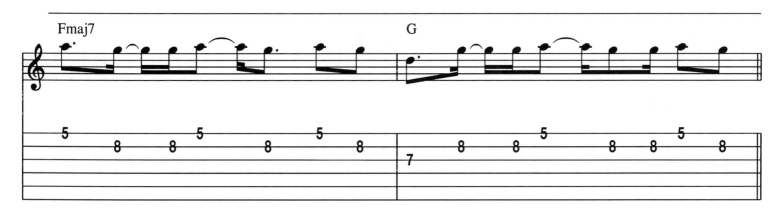

Interlude

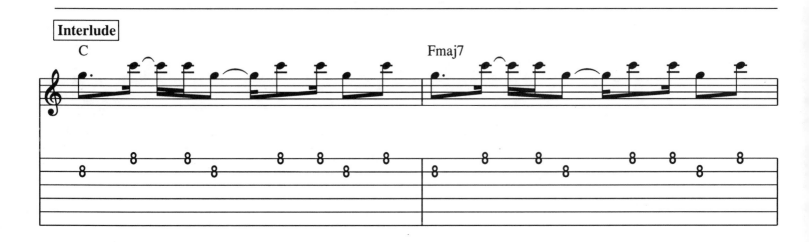

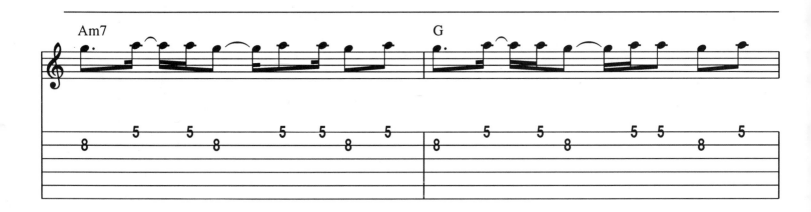

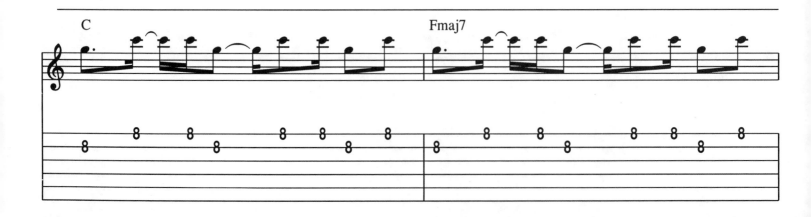

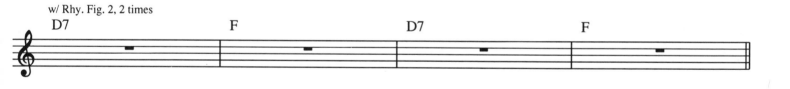

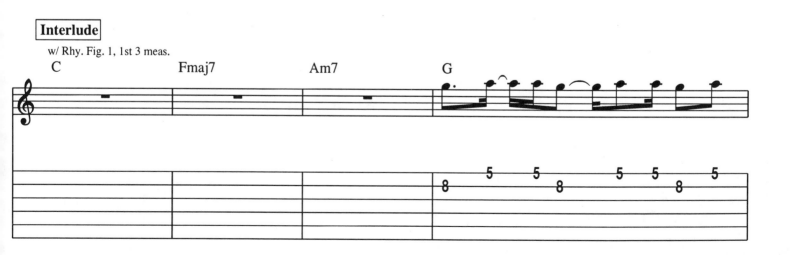

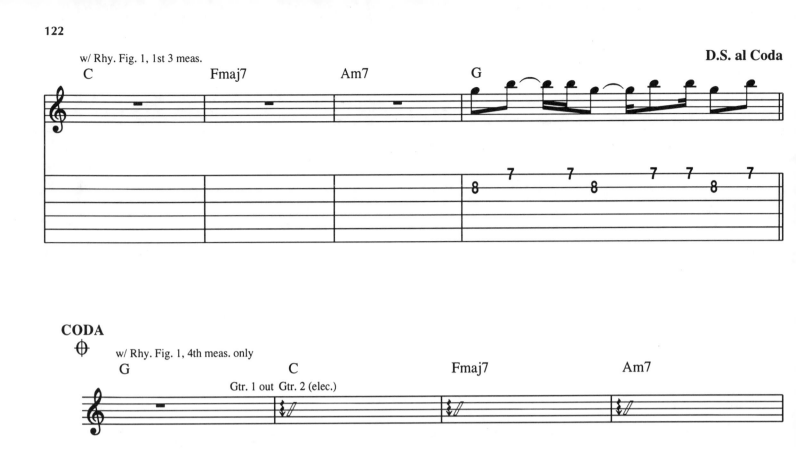

CODA

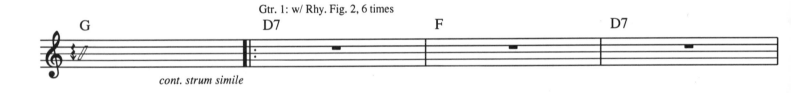

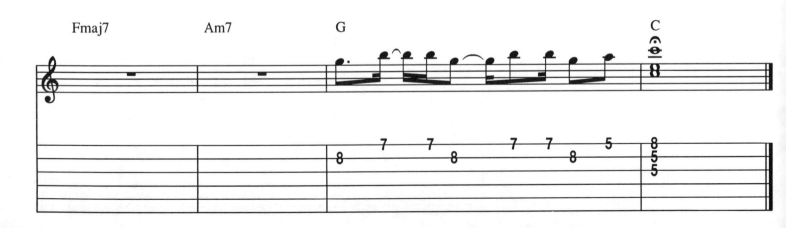

DRAWN TO THE RHYTHM
(Guitar Part)

Words and Music by
SARAH McLACHLAN

MCA music publishing

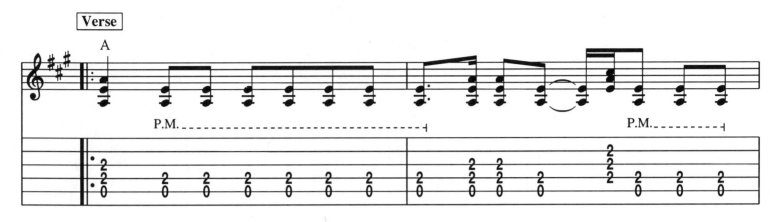

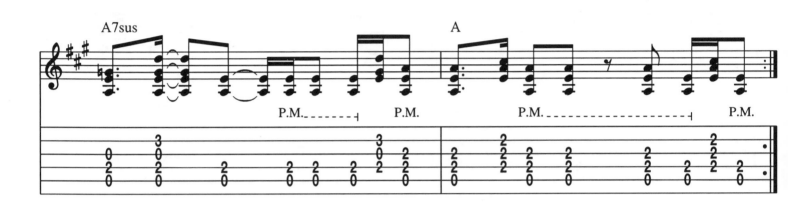

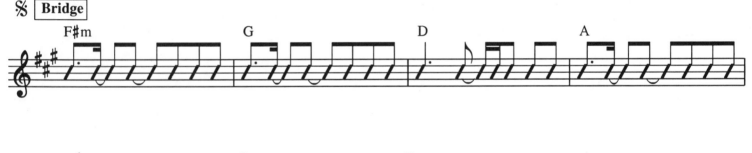

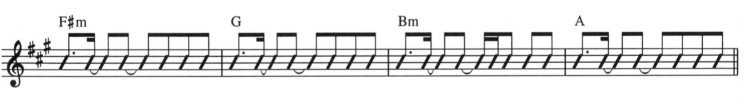

THE PATH OF THORNS (TERMS)
(Guitar Part)

Words and Music by
SARAH McLACHLAN

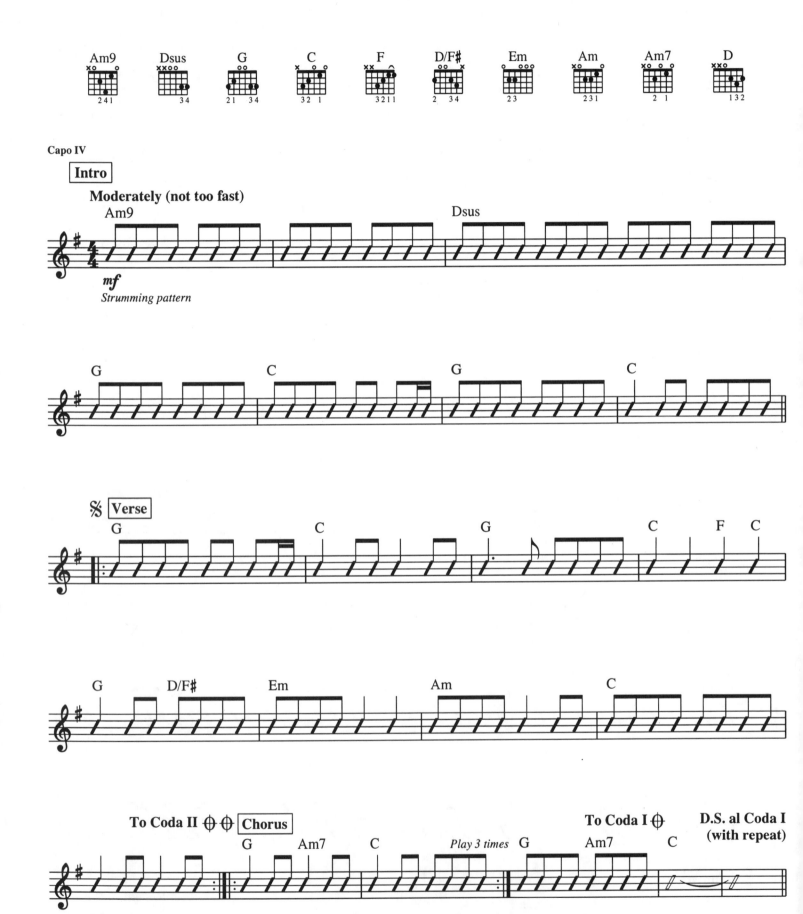

MCA music publishing

* pick strings just in front of bridge

I WILL NOT FORGET YOU

(Guitar Part)

Words and Music by SARAH McLACHLAN
and DARREN PHILLIPS

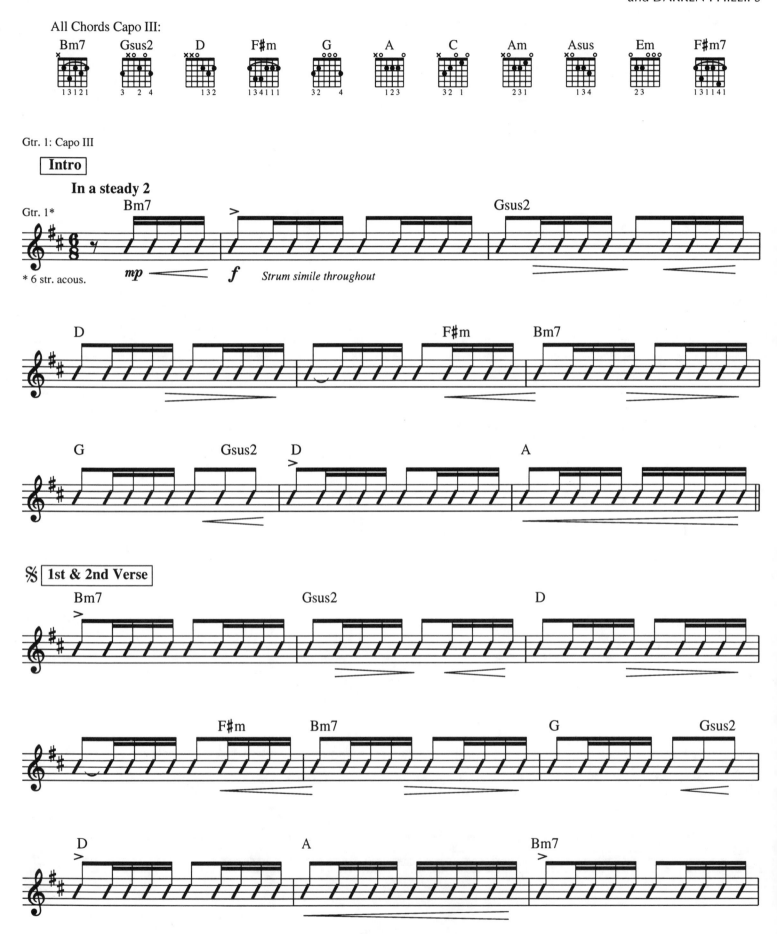

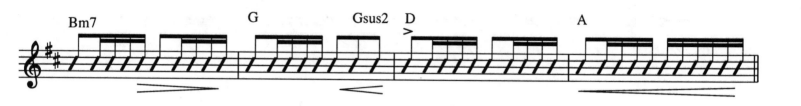

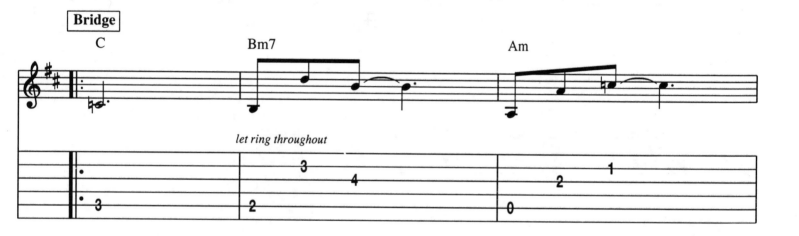

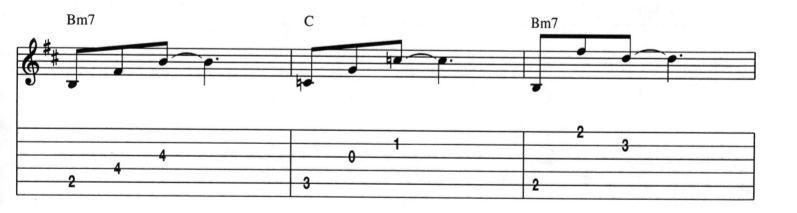

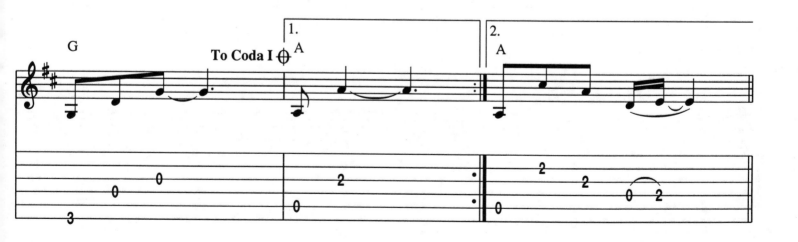

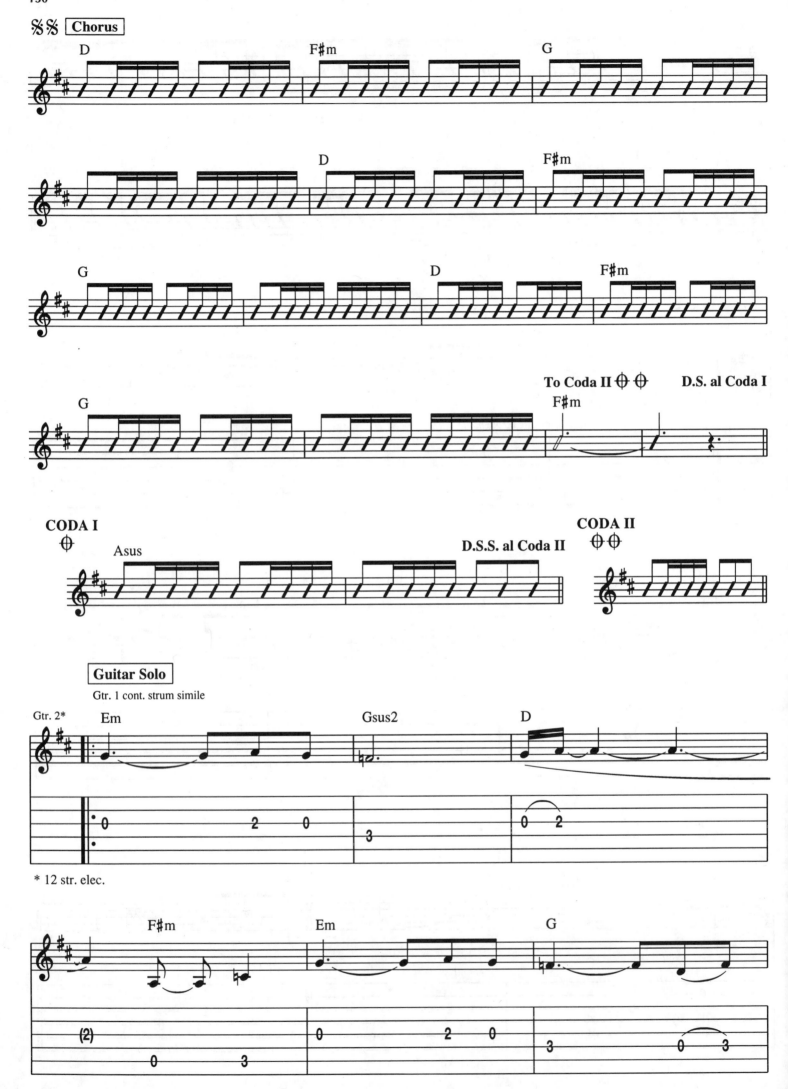

Chorus

LOST
(Guitar Part)

Words and Music by
SARAH McLACHLAN

All Chords Capo III:

Gtrs. 1 & 2, Capo III

*6-str. acous.

Instrumental

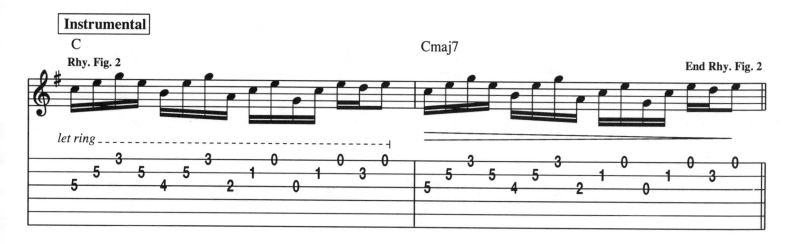

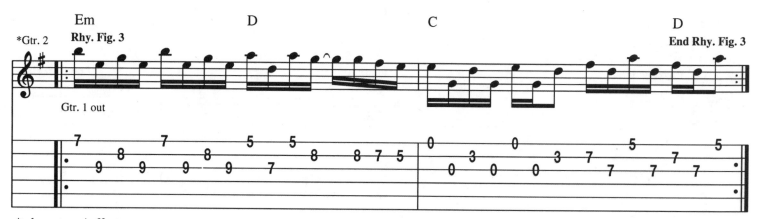

* elec. gtr. w/ effects

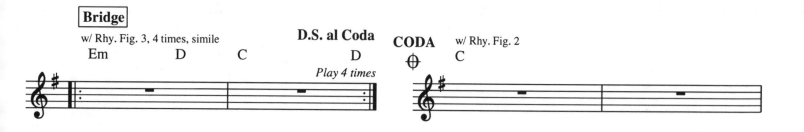

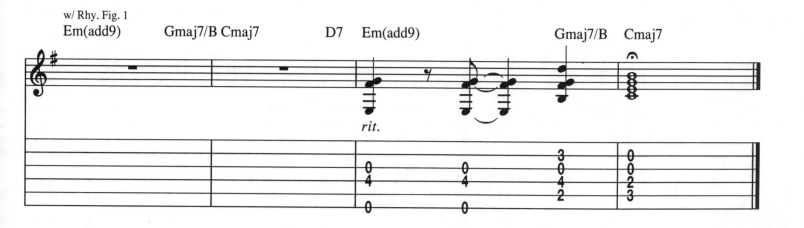

POSSESSION
(Guitar Part)

Words and Music by
SARAH McLACHLAN

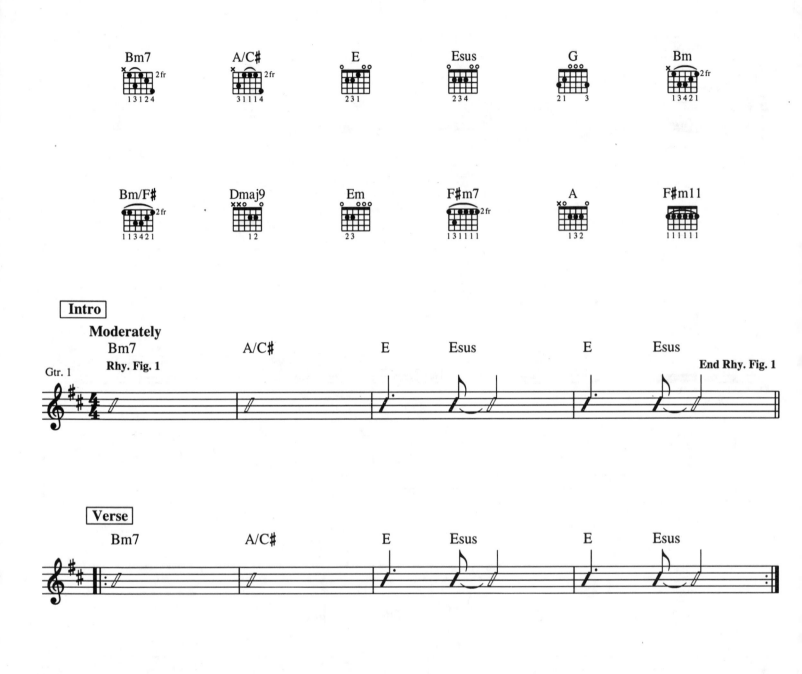

* elec. gtr. w/ dist.

WAIT
(Guitar Part)

Words and Music by
SARAH McLACHLAN

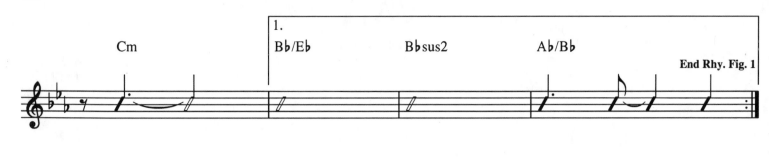

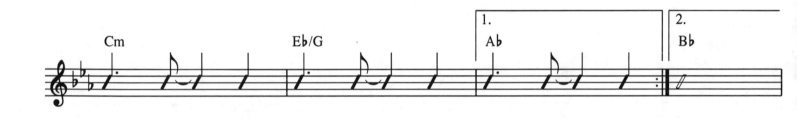

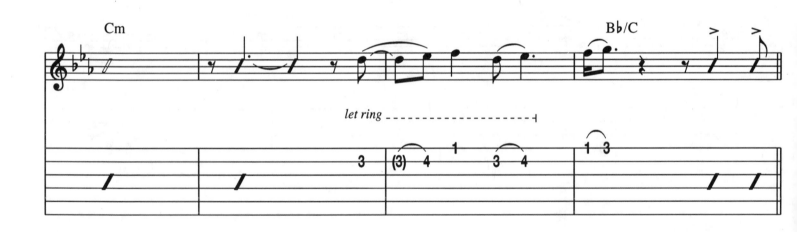

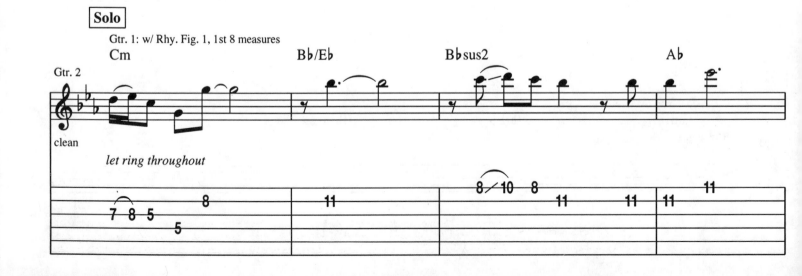

Outro

Gtr. 2: cont. improv. as in verse

Gtr. 1

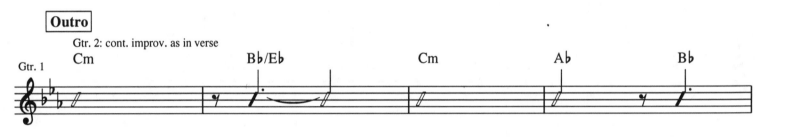

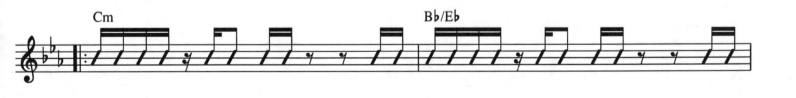

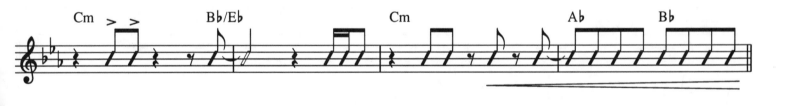

Repeat and Fade

GOOD ENOUGH
(Guitar Part)

Words and Music by
SARAH McLACHLAN

Guitar Solo

CIRCLE
(Guitar Part)

Words and Music by
SARAH McLACHLAN

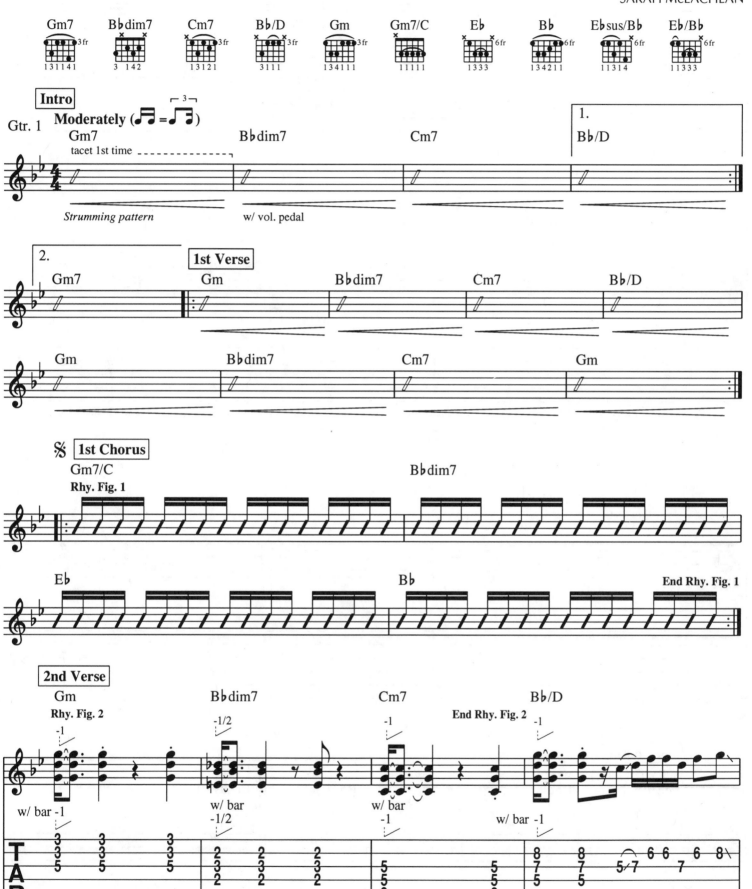

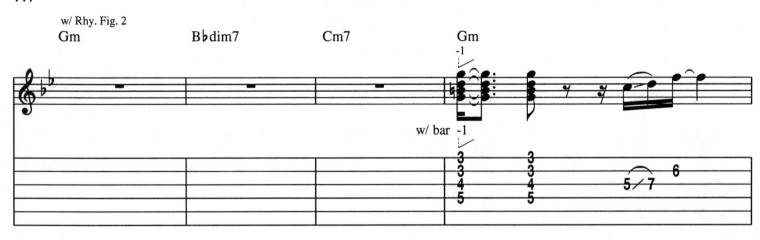

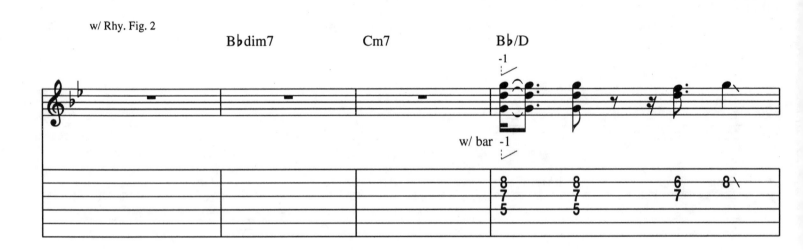

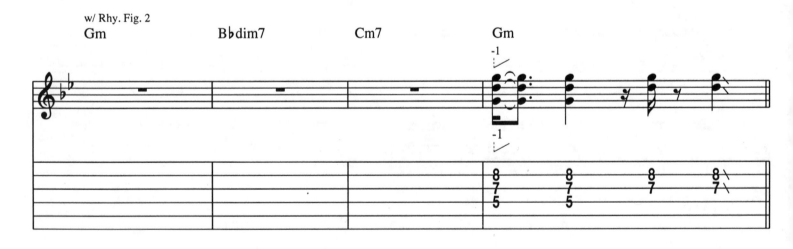

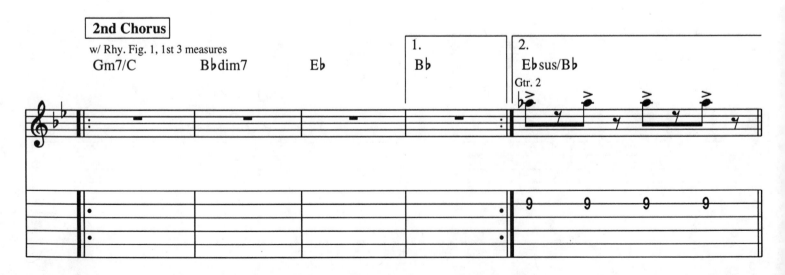

Guitar Solo

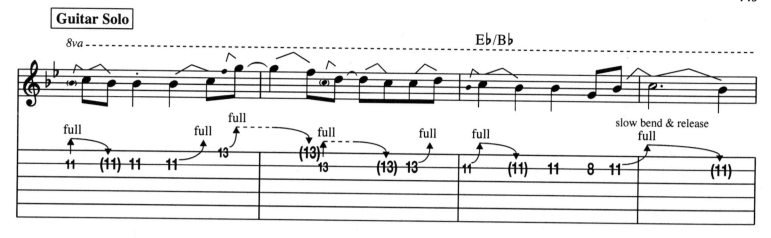

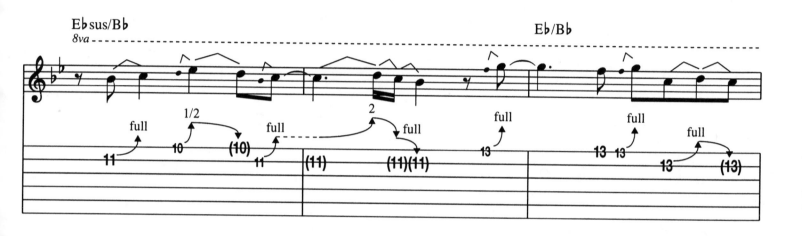

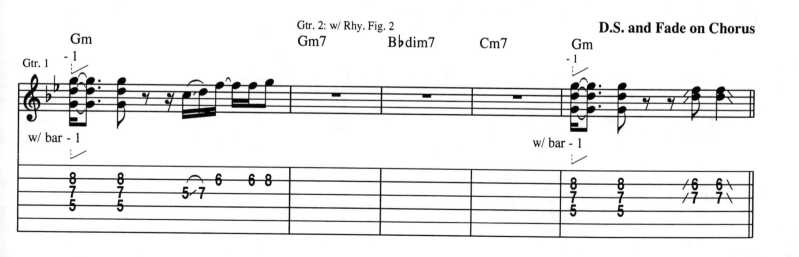

ELSEWHERE
(Guitar Part)

Words and Music by
SARAH McLACHLAN

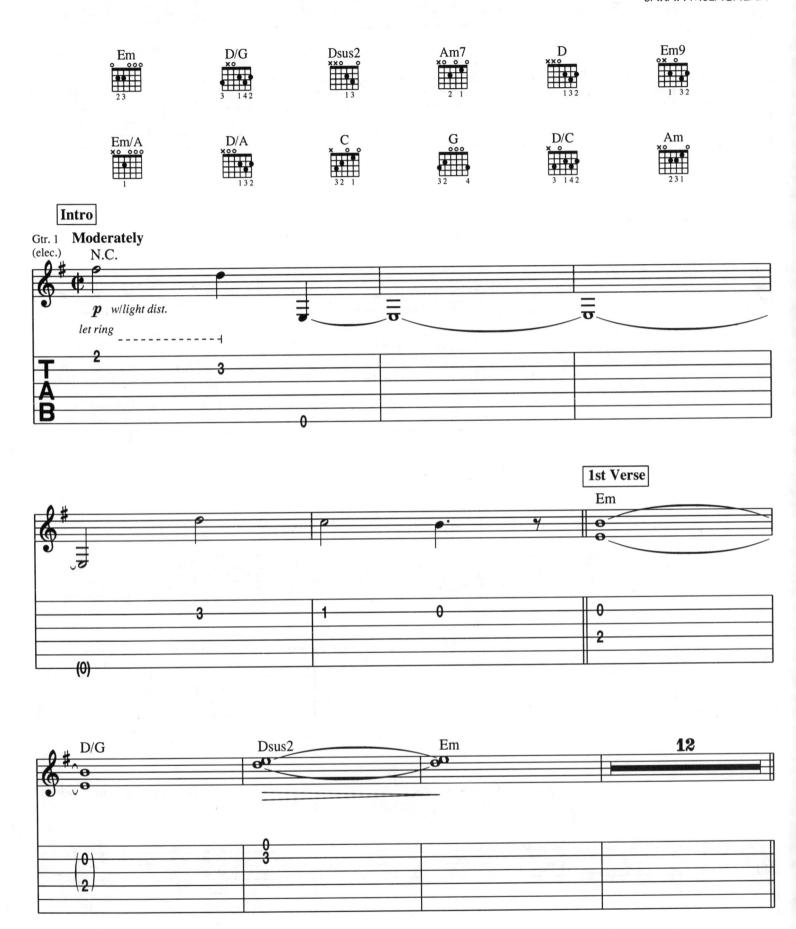

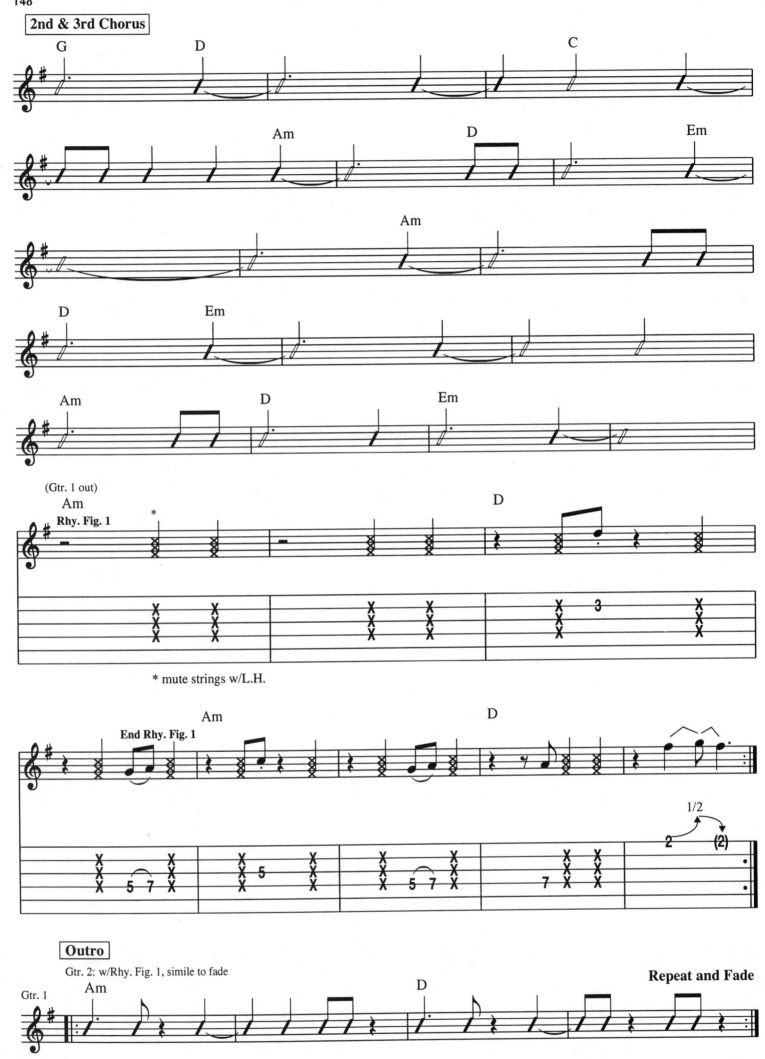

MARY
(Guitar Part)

Words and Music by
SARAH McLACHLAN

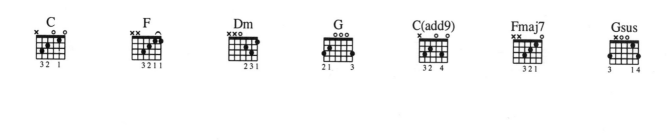

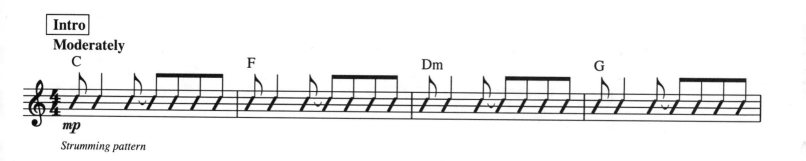

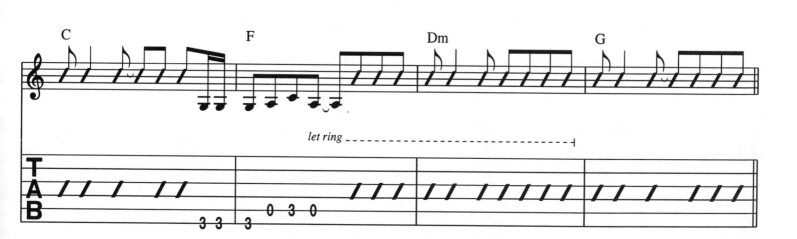

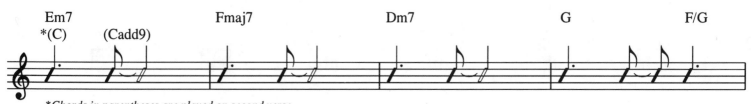

*Chords in parentheses are played on second verse.

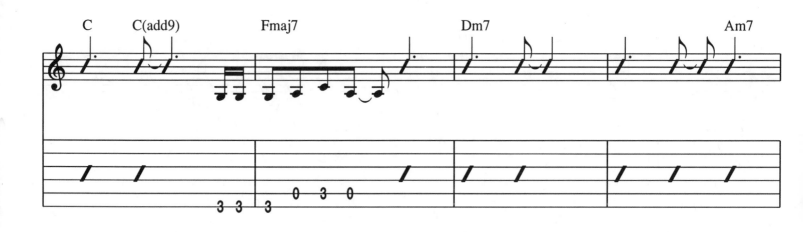

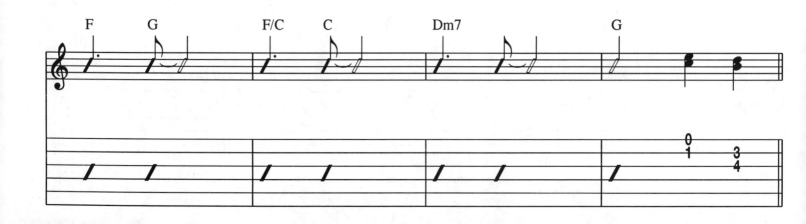

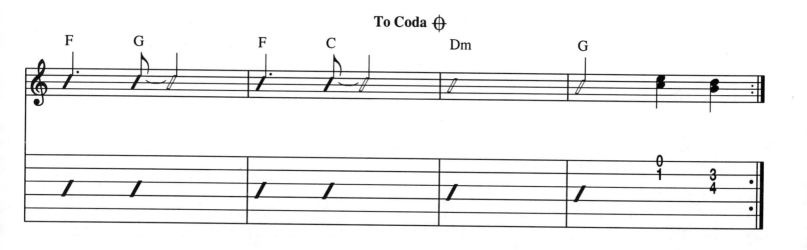

HOLD ON
(Guitar Part)

Words and Music by
SARAH McLACHLAN

1st Verse

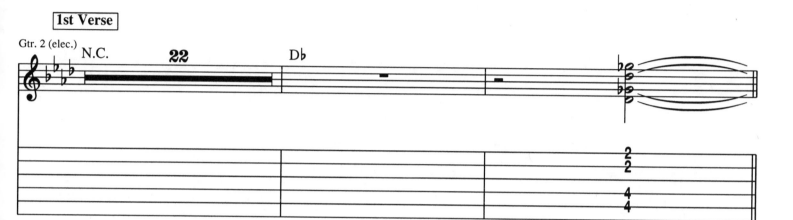

2nd Verse

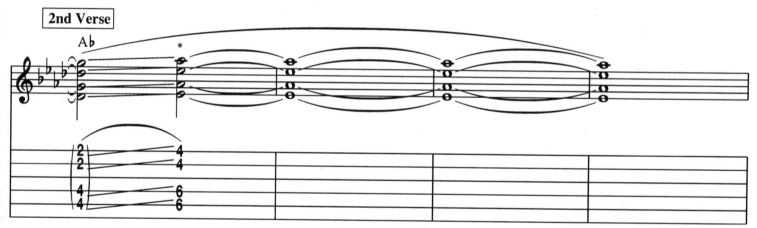

* Slide is produced by an effects
device on the recording,
but may be played as indicated.

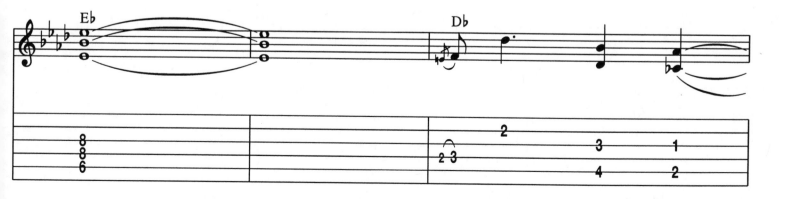

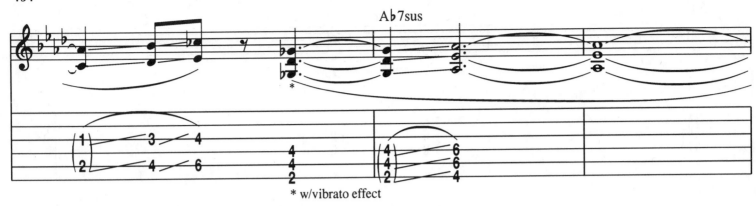

* w/vibrato effect

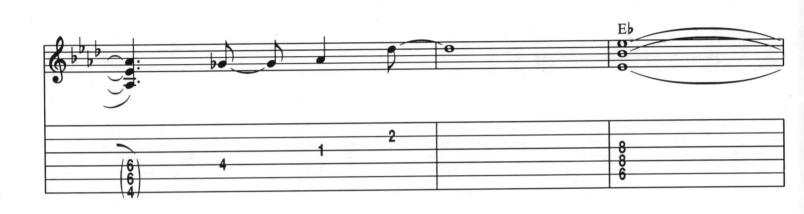

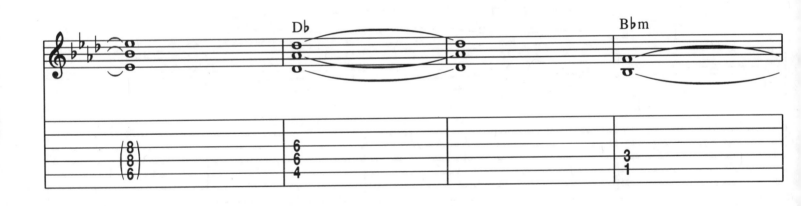

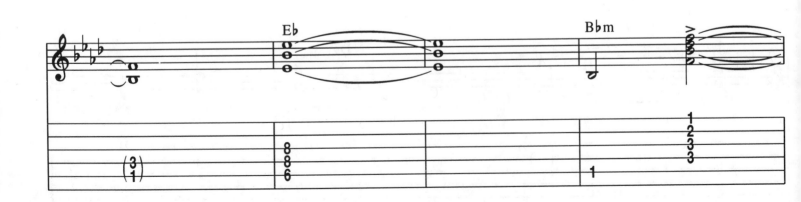

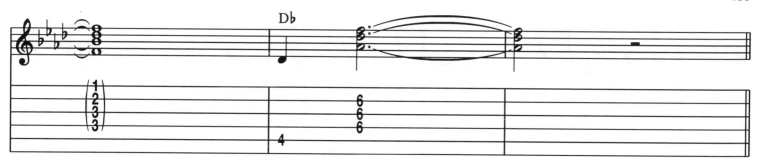

Chorus

Strumming pattern

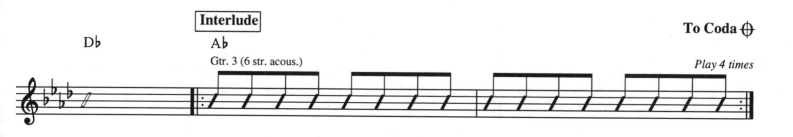

Interlude

To Coda ⊕

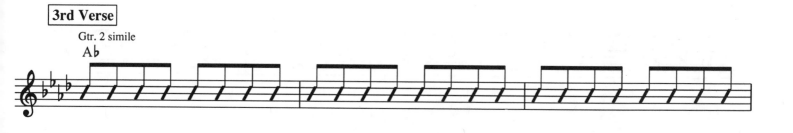

3rd Verse

156

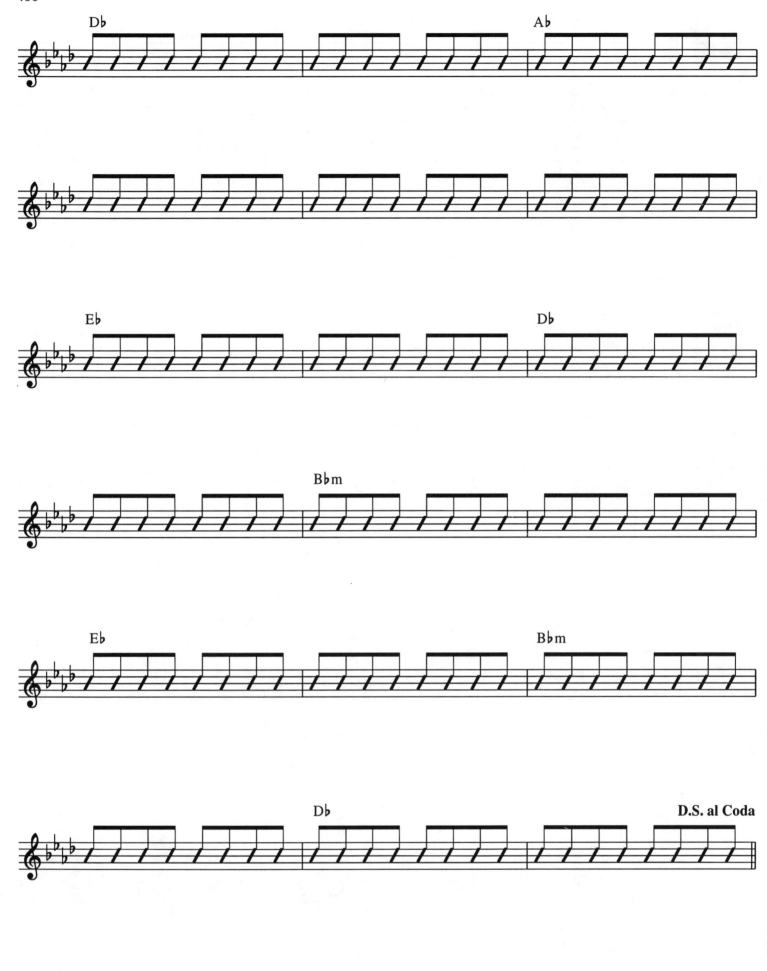

ICE
(Guitar Part)

Words and Music by
SARAH McLACHLAN

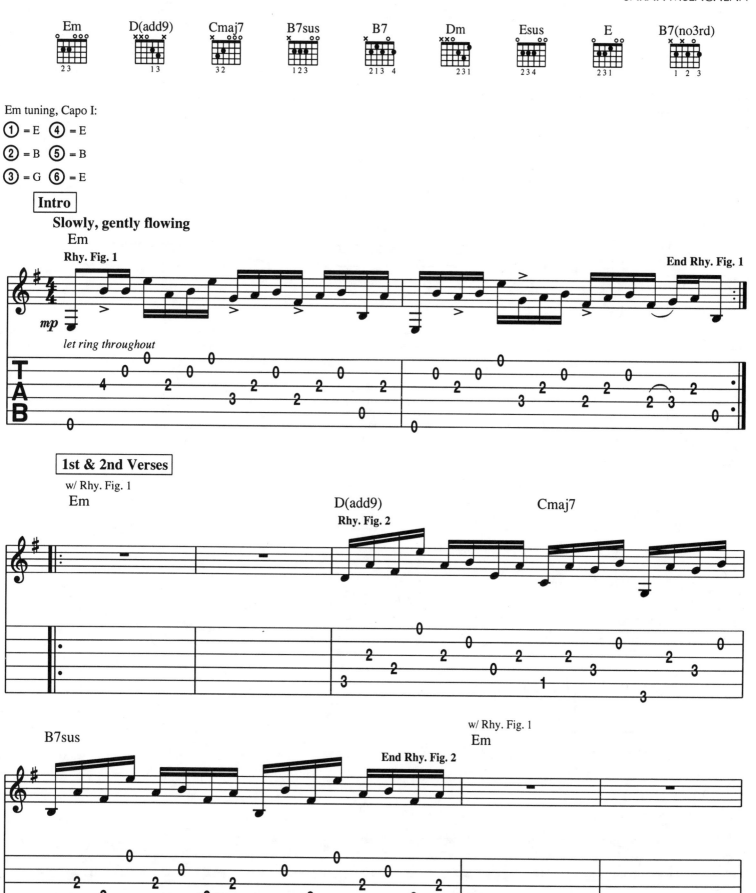

ICE CREAM
(Guitar Part)

Words and Music by
SARAH McLACHLAN

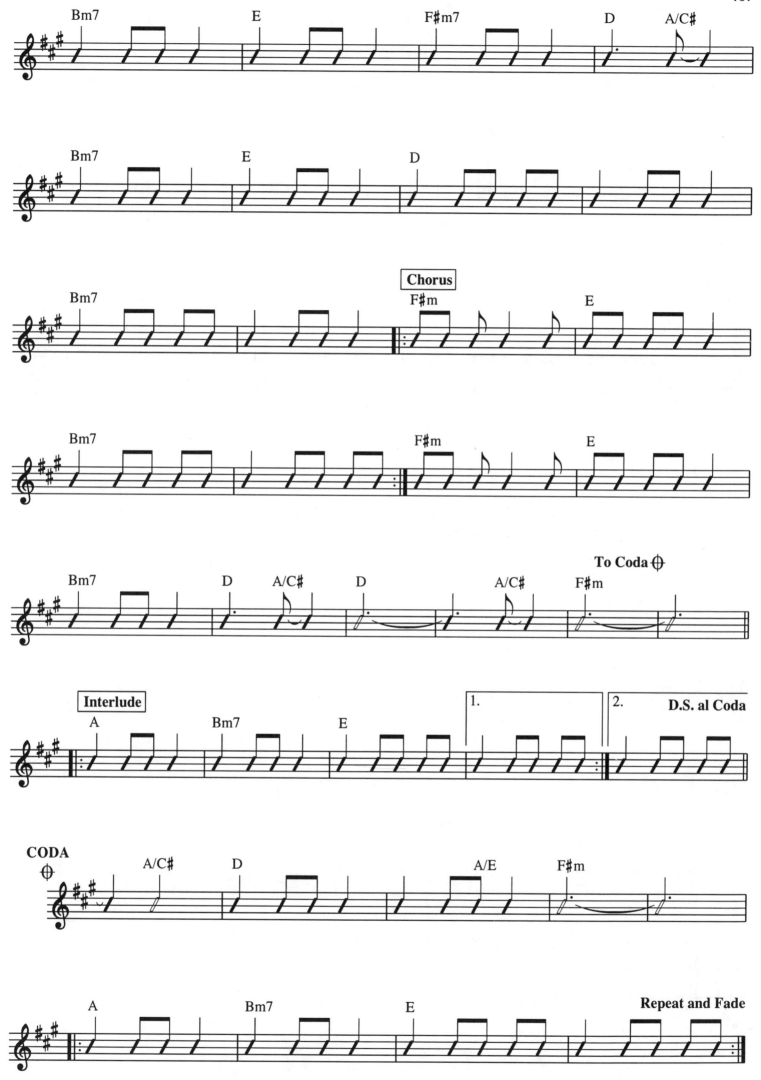

PLENTY
(Guitar Part)

Words and Music by
SARAH McLACHLAN

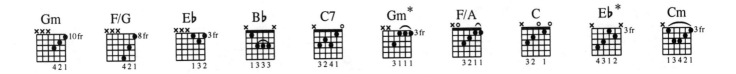

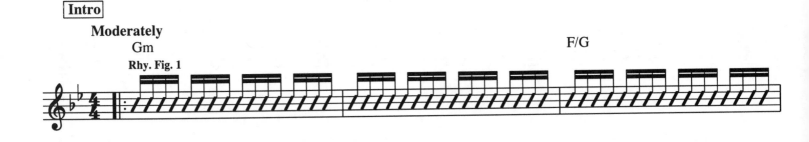

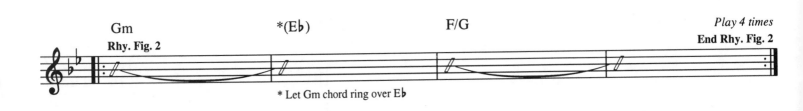

* Let Gm chord ring over Eb

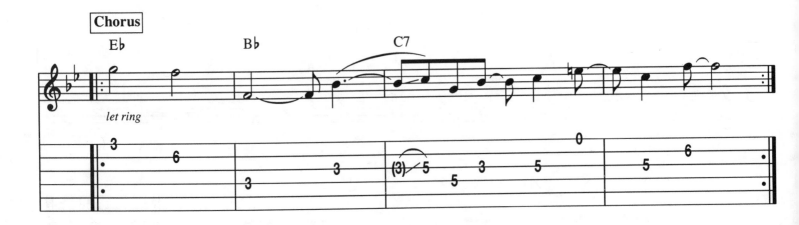

let ring

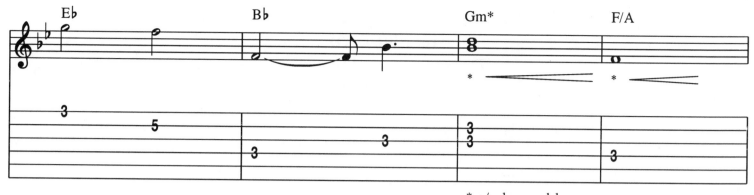

* w/volume pedal

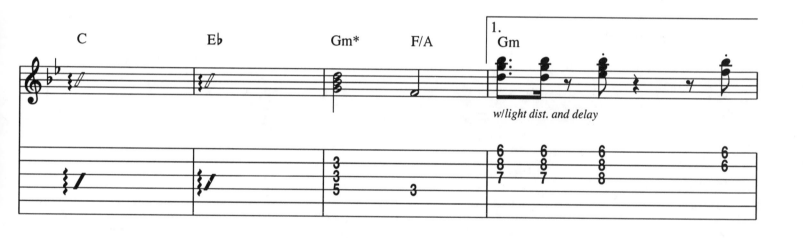

w/light dist. and delay

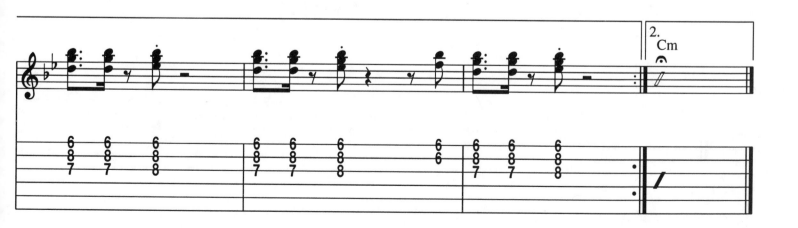

FUMBLING TOWARDS ECSTASY
(Guitar Part)

Words and Music by SARAH McLACHLAN
and PIERRE MARCHAND

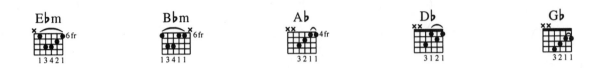

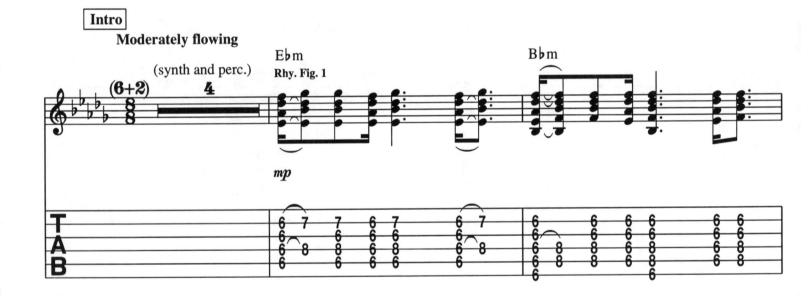

w/ Rhy. Fig. 1, 3 times

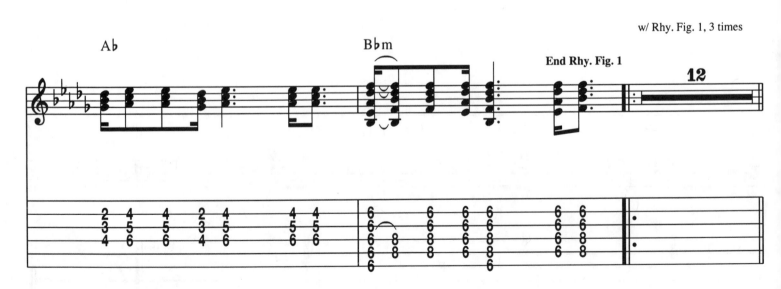

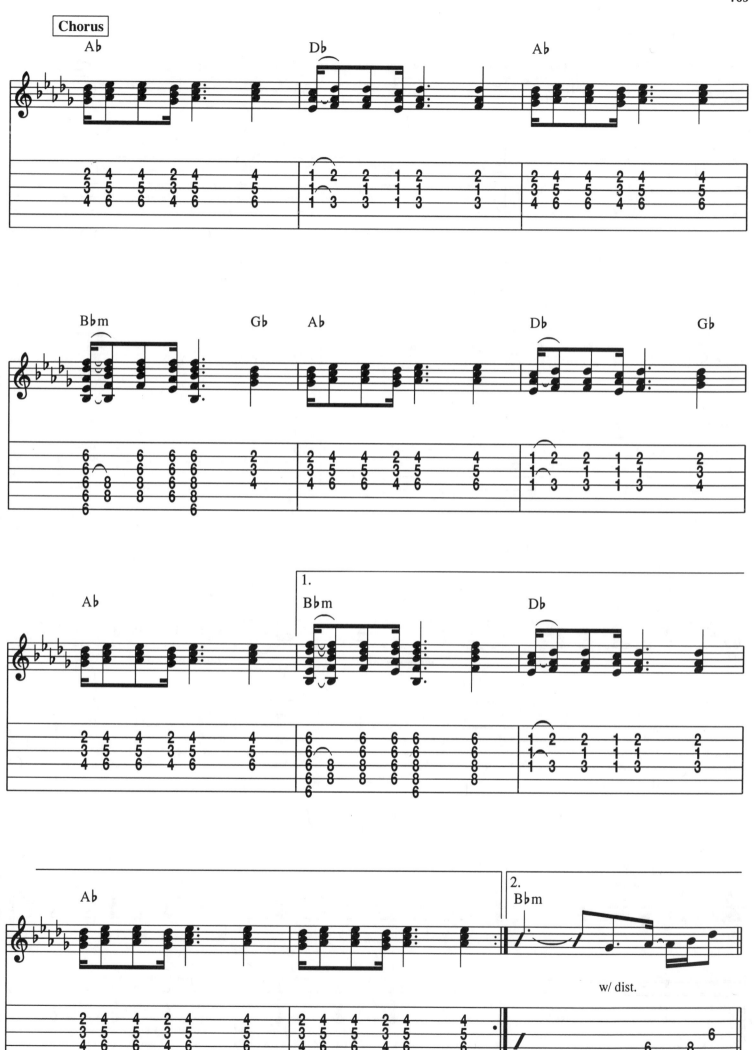

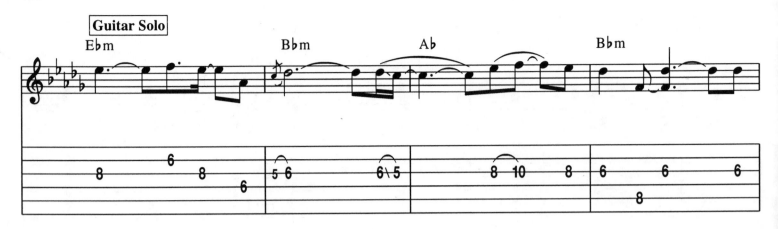

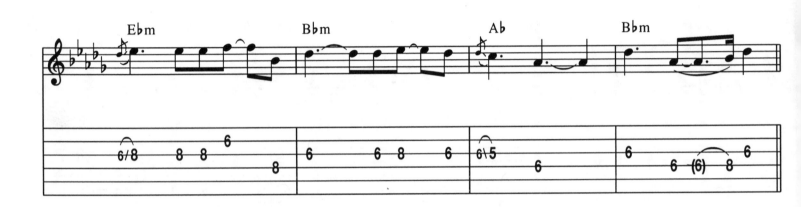

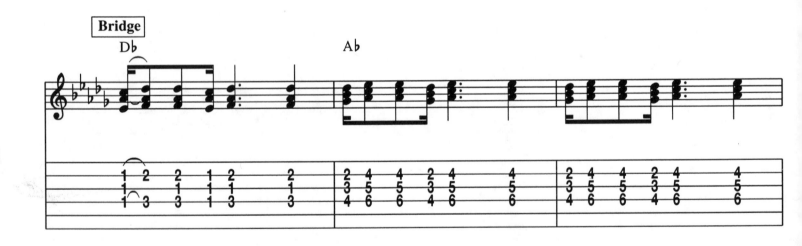

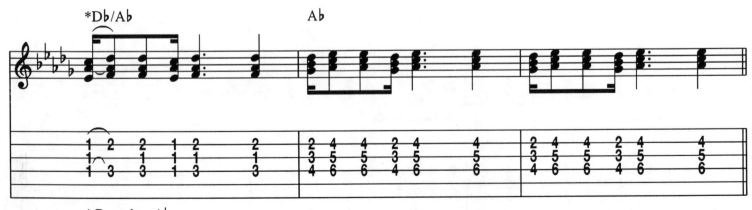

* Bass plays A♭

Chorus

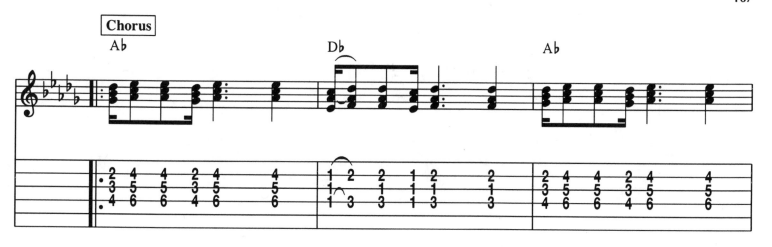

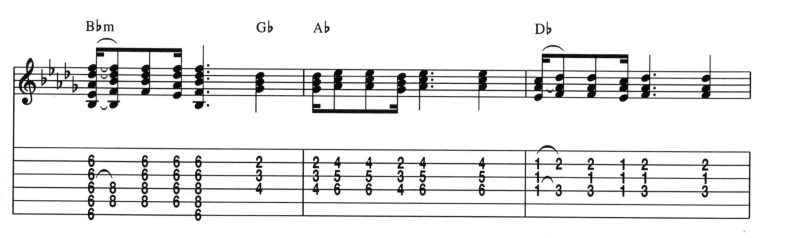

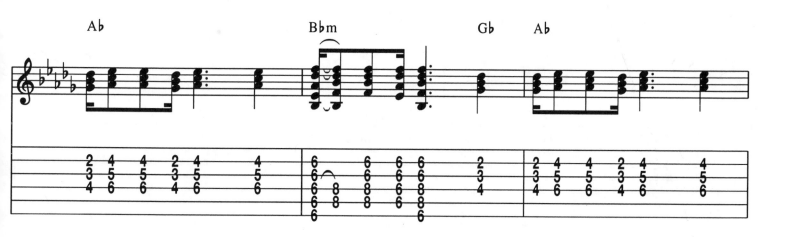

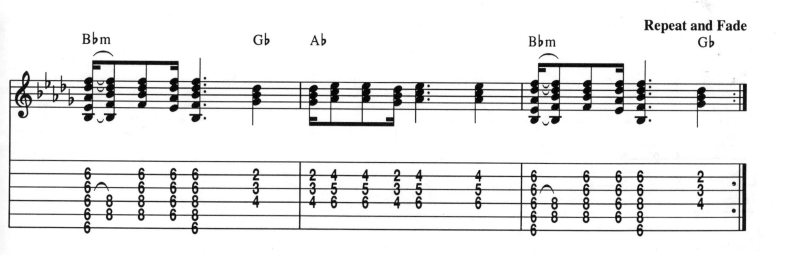

FEAR
(Guitar Part)

Words and Music by
SARAH McLACHLAN

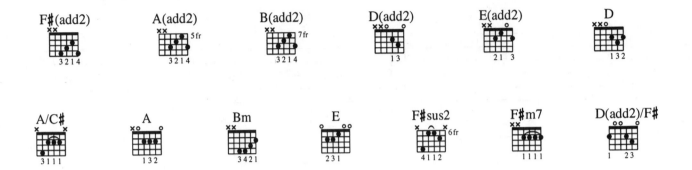

Guitar Solo

Moderately

F#sus2

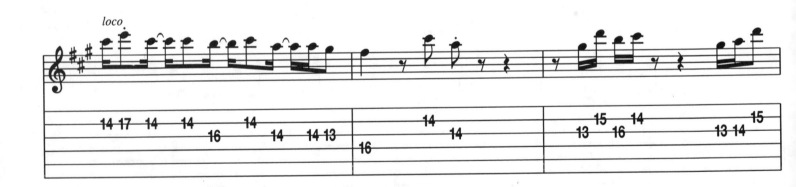